July '92

Dear Alistair & family,

Hope you can all come real soon and experience all this in person.

Best Wishes,

Leigh
George
Jordan
Ashleigh

PETRIGO'S
CALGARY
КАЛГАРИ
カルガリー

INTERNATIONAL EDITION

Calgary—more than just a dot on the map, not
just a city of concrete and steel—but a friend,
alive and pulsing, who has everything
dearest within.

Petrigo

1

PETRIGO'S
CALGARY

Forewords In:

ENGLISH

FRENCH

SPANISH

RUSSIAN

GERMAN

JAPANESE

PETRIGO'S
CALGARY
КАЛГАРИ
カルガリー

INTERNATIONAL EDITION

WALTER PETRIGO
M. Photog. Cr.; M.P.A.; F.R.P.S.

To the people of Calgary
who have made this city and book what it is—
reflection of our lives and efforts.

Petrigo

I.S.B.N. 0-921204-00-0

Photos processed by
West Canadian Color.

Translations by
Action Communications International

CENTURY PRESS (FOOTHILLS) INC.
Printed and bound in Canada

It was a hard day's ride. I could feel the grit of the dust under my teeth. I touched the side of my horse and in that dryness a small cloud of dust rose. It was time for the unit to stop and rest.

It was to be a normal stop, I thought, until I rode to the top of the hill to take a look at the area. It was beautiful. For a soldier who has seen and experienced much, who is not meant to understand more than the factual, who did not have time for poetry and beauty to accept as such, it was a moving sight. The Rockies were glittering under the rays of the setting sun, the waters of the Bow and Elbow framed a lush valley, the trees along the rivers offered refuge and peace.

We camped and felt at home.

It must have been an overwhelming feeling for those North West Mounted Police members who first saw and appreciated the area of the Canadian West which was to become the city of Calgary. I came to Calgary many years later — in 1951 — but I too felt the welcoming of this city. Without knowing it, I had found my place.

At that time, I had heard of Calgary for the first time only months before. A long trip by train from eastern Canada left plenty of time for my imagination to work. Over time I saw Calgary in my mind's eye as a vestige of old England, perhaps with an English landlord riding about his fields overseeing his workers. I also have to admit I imagined a bit of the old West too. I did not know what to expect.

What I found when I stepped off the train were simple things — more smiles, or little problems with everyday things, such as how to open the cream container in the first Calgary restaurant I visited. Otherwise, Calgary didn't seem that different from other cities the world over.

Now, to me, Calgary is home, and it's like no other place on earth. If you ask me what makes this city unique, I would answer that it is an unfair question because our language is not rich enough to define all those sensitive feelings that an individual has about his home. To me, Calgary is exceptional just because it is Calgary — a blend of people, of the mountains and prairies, of yesterday and tomorrow. When I blend all these attributes, I have Calgary.

I see Calgary as perhaps the most promising and vibrant city in Canada because it has for a foundation a bit of the hardship, a bit of the innocence of growing up spontaneously, without a sterile plan. First-hand experience is usually the hardest, and most Calgarians have blended the sweat of that first experience into the environment they call home.

Like people, cities are also old and young. Calgary is like a youngster growing, a youngster who is himself surprised with his own newly discovered strength and potential. Calgary is a youth who has outgrown his pants — the cuffs are somewhere between the ankles and the knees. But the head of this youth is high, he is proud and looks forward. And somehow even through the change of times which we are witnessing now, I don't think this young city will ever have to look back because it contains the hope and potential of youth everywhere.

To portray a city by showing only its buildings is really to ignore the most important part of that city — the people and their reactions, their efforts which have created all those structures. I think it's better to know the need for those structures than just see the structures by themselves.

While it is true that people are the most important asset of any city, it is also true that people do not come as giants. They come as small units, fitting together to create a whole that is more than the parts could ever have imagined. Thus the child ... the old man ... they all contribute in unexpected ways to making the structure of a city.

Calgary has a current of reality which comes from the earth and is deeply rooted. Cities are supposed to grow in certain prescribed ways, but Calgary hasn't. Individuals have made it what it is ... fluently, without strain, without pattern, without that division between what a city is supposed to be and what it is. Calgary is what it is.

It is not a cowboy town, in spite of its reputation. We like to hang onto our heritage, and the Stampede is a reflection of that desire, so everybody turns into a cowboy for ten days or so in the summer. The western boots that we wear and the cowboy hat reflect a want in our minds, which has no connection with practicality. We want to be western, at least for awhile, but time has wrought its changes.

But that Stampede gives us a feeling of the past. You can walk behind the chutes in the infield and find there the foundation of Calgary. You can still feel and hear the sturdy talk of the descendants of the pioneers, you can find the roughness which has built this country. There also you can find the chivalry of the past — a tall cowboy tips his hat in apology to someone he's just pushed. This is not the Calgary of today, the metropolis of commerce and agriculture. This is the past spilling into the present.

Calgary cannot be dissected from its surrounding area because the surrounding area also makes it what it is. Mountains, prairies, oil fields, even the smell of the fertile soil — all these assets are Calgary.

Calgary has the best of both worlds — city and country. There is no division. And because the city is so rich in its resources, it lets anyone reach for whatever he wants to do. As a photographer, I can find the variety so necessary to feed an artistic curiosity — a variety of people, variety of architecture, variety of landscape.

In this book, I have tried to reflect that variety, a variety which also includes the stages of development which this city has gone through. I want the book to be real, and to do that, I can't forget what Calgary has left by the wayside while growing up, because that also has contributed to today. Without debris, you do not have a structure.

Many times the photographs in this collection will silently speak for themselves, reflecting what I felt or understood when I myself was part of the photograph. It is their responsibility to speak for me from now on, and if they do their job well, as I hope they do, other people will share my understanding of this city. If that happens, then I have succeeded in presenting Petrigo's Calgary.

C'était la fin d'un longue randonnée. J'avais un goût de poussiére dans la bouche. J'ai touché le flanc de mon cheval et dans la sécheresse, un petit nuage de poussière s'est élevé. Il était temps de nous arrêter et de nous reposer.

J'ai pensé que ce serait un arrêt normal mais lorsque j'ai atteint le sommet de la colline pour jeter un coup d'oeil à la région, c'était superbe. Pour un soldat qui avait beaucoup vu et appris, qui n'était pas supposé comprendre plus que les faits, qui n'avait pas de temps pour la poésie et la beauté en tant que telles, c'était un paysage émouvant. Les Rocheuses scintillaient sous les derniers rayons du soleil couchant, les eaux des rivières Bow et Elbow encadraient une vallée luxuriante, les arbres le long des rivières offraient refuge et paix.

Nous avons campé et nous nous sommes sentis chez nous.

Ça a dû être pareil pour les membres de la Gendarmerie Royale du Nord Ouest lorsqu'ils ont vu et apprécié pour la première fois cette région de l'ouest du Canada qui allait devenir la ville de Calgary. Je suit arrivé à Calgary bien des années plus tard — en 1951 — mais moi aussi, j'ai ressenti l'accueil chaleureux de cette ville. Sans le savoir, j'avais trouvé mon endroit de prédilection.

A cette époque, il n'y avait que quelques mois que j'avais entendu parler de Calgary pour la première fois. Au cours du long voyage en train à partir de l'est du Canada, j'avais laissé courir mon imagination. Dans mon esprit, je voyais Calgary comme un vestige de la vieille Angleterre, avec peut être un propriétaire terrien anglais parcourant ses terres à cheval et surveillant ses employés. Je dois admettre aussi que j'avais imaginé un peu ce que pouvait être l'ouest. Je ne savais pas à quoi m'attendre.

Ce que je trouvai en descendant du train fut tout simple, des gens plus souriants et les mêmes petits problèmes quotidiens tel que comment me servir du pot à crème dans le premier restaurant de Calgary que je visitai. Autrement, Calgary n'était pas différente des autres grandes villes à travers le monde.

Maintenant, mon foyer, c'est Calgary et ça ne ressemble à aucun autre endroit sur terre. Si vous me demandez ce qui rend cette ville unique, je peux vous répondre que ce n'est pas une question juste parce que notre langue n'est pas assez riche pour définir tous les sentiments sensibles qu'un individu éprouve à l'égard de son foyer. Pour moi, Calgary est exceptionnelle justement parce que c'est Calgary — un mélange de gens, de montagnes et de prairie, d'hier et de demain. Quand j'ai bien mélangé toutes ces données, alors j'ai Calgary.

Je considère Calgary comme étant peut être la ville la plus prometteuse et la plus vibrante du Canada parce qu'elle a pour base un peu des temps difficile et un peu de l'innocence d'une croissance spontanée sans plan stérile. L'expérience de première main est généralement la plus difficile et la plupart des calgariens ont répandu la sueur de cette première expérience dans l'environnement qu'ils appellent leur foyer.

Comme les gens, les villes sont vieilles ou jeunes. Calgary est comme un enfant en train de grandir, en enfant surpris de découvrir sa propre force et son potentiel. Calgary est comme un jeune garçon dont les pantalons sont devenus trop courts, les pans sont quelque part entre les chevilles et les genoux. Mais le jeune garçon garde la tête haute, il est fier et regarde vers l'avenir. Et d'une manière ou d'une autre, malgré les changements dont nous sommes les témoins maintenant, je ne pense pas que cette ville récente ait à regarder en arrière parce qu'elle détient l'espoir et le potentiel de la jeunesse.

Montrer une ville en révélant seulement ses édifices est vraiment ignorer la partie la plus importante de cette ville — les gens et leurs réactions, leurs efforts qui ont créé toutes ces structures. Je pense qu'il vaut mieux connaître le besoin de ces structures que juste regarder ces structures par elles-mêmes.

Alors qu'il est exact que les gens représentent l'apport le plus important de tout ville, il est vrai également que les gens n'y arrivent pa en tant que géants. Ils viennent en tant que petites unités, s'adaptant ensemble pour créer un tout qui représente beaucoup plus que ce qui avait été envisagé. Ainsi, l'enfant . . .

le vieil homme . . . ils contribuent tous de manière inattendue à la structure d'une ville.

Calgary possède un courant de réalité qui vient de la terre et qui est profondément enraciné. Les villes doivent s'agrandir suivant des plans biens définis mais cela, Calgary ne l'a pas fait. Les gens l'ont fait ce qu'elle est . . . facilement, sans contrainte, sans plan, sans cette division entre ce qu'une ville doit être et ce qu'elle est. Calgary est telle quelle.

Ce n'est pas une ville de vachers, en dépit de sa réputation. Nous aimons garder notre patrimoine et le Stampede reflète ce désir, donc, chacun se transforme en cow-boy pendant dix jours ou plus en été. Les bottes que nous portons et le chapeau de cow-boy reflètent une expression de notre esprit qui n'a aucune attache avec l'aspect pratique. Nous voulons appartenir à l'ouest, au moins pendant un certain temps, mais le temps a façonné les changements.

Mais le Stampede nous donne un sentiment du passé. Vous pouvez marcher derrière les rampes à bétail dans les champs et trouver là la base de Calgary. Vous pouvez toujours ressentir et écouter le bavardage hardi des descendants des pionniers, vous pouvez retrouver cette rudesse qui a construit ce pays. Là aussi, vous pouvez retrouver la courtoisie du passé — un grand cow-boy soulève son chapeau pour s'excuser auprès de quelqu'un qu'il a bousculé. Ce n'est pas le Calgary d'aujourd'hui, la métropole du commerce et de l'agriculture. C'est le passé qui rejaillit sur le présent.

Calgary ne peut pas être séparé de la région environnante, parce que c'est cette région qui l'a faite telle qu'elle est. Les montagnes, les prairies, les champs pétroliers, même l'odeur du sol fertile, tous ces attributs constituent Calgary.

Calgary a le meilleur de deux mondes, la ville et la campagne. Il n'y a pas de division. Et parce que cette ville a de riches ressources, cela permet à chacun d'essayer de faire ce qu'il veut. En tant que photographe, je peux trouver la variété si nécessaire à nourrir la curiosité artistique — une variété de gens, une variété d'architecture, une variété de paysages.

Dans ce livre, j'ai essayé de refléter cette variété, une variété qui inclut aussi les étapes du développement que la ville a subi. Je veux que ce livre soit réel et pour atteindre ce but, je ne peux pas oublier ce que Calgary a laissé de côté en grandissant, parce que cela aussi contribue à aujourd'hui. Sans débris, vous n'avez pas de structure.

Très souvent, les photographies de cette collection parleront d'elles-mêmes, silencieusement, reflètant ce que j'ai ressenti ou compris quand moi-même je faisais parti de la photographie. C'est leur responsabilité de parler en mon nom maintenant et si elles y réussissent aussi bien que je l'espère, d'autres personnes partageront ma compréhension. Si c'est ce qui se passe, alors j'aurai réussi à représenter le Calgary de Petrigo.

Fué una cabalgada larga. Notaba el sabor de la arena en la boca. Toqué a mi caballo en un lado, y en el medio de la sequedad levanté una nubecilla de polvo. Era hora de parar y descansar.

Pensé que iba a ser una parada normal hasta que subi a la colina para observar la zona. El paisaje era precioso; una vista emocionante para un soldada con mucho mundo, pero que no esta entrenado para entender nada mas que lo factual y que no tuvo tiempo para admirar poesia y belleza. Las Rocosas resplandecian bajo los rayos del sol poniente, las aguas de Bow y Elbow formaban un valle lozano y los árboles a lo largo de los rios ofrecìan refugio y tranquilidad.

Acampamos y nos sentimos en casa.

Debieron de ser miembros de la Policia Montada del Noroeste los que primero vieron y apreciaron esta zona del Oeste de Canadá la cual más tarde iba a ser la ciudad de Cálgary. Yo vine muchos años mas tarde, en 1951, pero también noté la acogedora bienvenida de esta ciudad. Sin darme cuenta habia encontrado mu lugar.

Unos meses antes de aquella vez no habia oido de Cálgary. Un viaje largo en tren desde el este de Cánada dió amplio tiempo para formarme una idea en mi cabeza. Me imaginé Cálgary como un vestigio de mi querida Inglaterra, quizás con un terrateniente inglés cabalgando en sus campos y observando a sus trabajadores. Debo admitir que tambien me imaginé algo del Oeste Américano. Realmente no sabia que esperar.

Cuando me bajé del trén encontré cosas sencillas, gente agradable y pequeños problemas, como por ejemplo el abrir un recipiente de leche en el primer restaurante que estuve. Por otro lado, Cálgary no parecia ni mas ni menos diferente que cualquier otra gran ciudad en cualquier parte del mundo.

Ahora, Cálgary es mi hogar, y no hay otro lugar en este mundo que se le compare. Si me pregunta por qué esta ciudad es única, le contestaria que su pregunta no es justa puesto que nuestro idioma no es suficientemente rico como para definir los sentimientos que se pueden tener a su hogar. Para mi, Cálgary es excepcional solo porque es Cálgary, una variedad de gente, montañas y praderas, pasado y futuro.

Veo a Cálgary como la ciudad de más vida y con el mejor futuro de todo Canada, porque tiene raices, entereza y la inocencia de crecer espontaneamente sin un plan estéril. Los primeros dias son normalmente los más duros, la mayor parte de los Calgarianos han mezclado el sudor y el trabajo de los primeros dias en el circulo que llaman su casa.

Los mismo que la gente, las ciudades tambien son viejas y jóvenes. Cálgary es como un adolescente que está creciendo, que él mismo esta sorprendido con la fuerza y el potencial que acaba de descubrir. Cálgary es igual que un joven al que los pantalones le han quedado pequeños, los bajos estan por alguna parte entre los tobillos y las rodillas, pero es esbelto, orgulloso y mira al futuro. Y mismo con todos los cambios por los que ahora estamos pasando, no creo que esta joven ciudad nunca mire al pasado porque se le ve confianza y juventud por todos lados.

Mostrar a una ciudad enseñando únicamente sus edificios, realmente es ignorar la parte más importante de dicha ciudad; la gente y sus reacciones y los esfuerzos que han creado esas estructuras. En mi opinión es mejor tener conocimiento de la necesidad de esas estructuras que el verlas.

El hecho de que la gente es el mejor valor que cualquier ciudad puede tener, es cierto; tambien es cierto que sus habitantes no son gigantes. Son unidades pequeñas, compenetrándose unas con otras a fin de crear algo que ninguna de esas unidades podia haber imaginado ella sola. Desde el niño hasta el anciano todos contibuyen en formas inesperadas a hacer la estructura de la ciudad.

La realidad de Cálgary esta bien sentada. Se supone que las ciudades han de crecer en una forma muy planificada, pero Cálgary no lo ha hecho. La gente ha hecho a Cálgary como es . . . fluente, sin tirantez, sin patrón y sin aquella división entre que marca lo que una ciudad debe ser y lo que es. Cálgary es los que es, Cálgary.

Pese a su reputación, no es una ciudad de vaqueros. Nos gusta guardar nuestro pasado, y La Estampida es en reflejo de ese deseo, durante el verano la mayoria de sus habitantes se convierten en vaqueros por aldredor de diez dias. Las botas y el sombrero de vaquero reflejan el deseo de nuestra mente, que no tiene conexión con lo práctico. Queremos vivir al estilo del Oeste, al menos por un rato, pero el tiempo ha traido consigu sus cambios.

Con todo, La Estampida nos da un retrato del pasado. Puede caminar en las cuadras y en los campos y encontrar los cimientos de Cálgary. Puede sentir y oir el habla vigorosa de los descendientes de los pioneros, y encontrar la aspereza que ha formado este lugar. Tambien encontrará la caballerosidad del pasado, un vaquero alto se quita su sombrero para pedir perdón a alguien con el que ha tropezado. Este no es El Cálgary de hoy, la métropolis de comercio y agricultura. Es el pasado mostrándose a traves del presente.

Cálgary tampoco puede separarse de la zona que lo rodea, porque esa area le hace lo que es. Montañas, praderas, campos petroliferos y mismo el olor de tierra fertil; todos esos valores son Cálgary.

Cálgary tiene lo mejor de dos mundos, ciudad y campo. No existe división alguna. Teniendo en cuenta que la ciudad es tan rica en recursos, permite que cualquiera consiga lo que desea. Como fotógrafo, puedo encontrar la variedad necesaria para alimentar mi curiosidad artistica, variedad de gente, variedad de arquetectura, como tambien variedad paisaje.

He tratado de reflejar dicha variedad en este libro, una variedad que tambien incluye algunos pasajes del desarrollo que esta ciudad ha experimentado. Quiero que este libro sea real, y para hacerlo no puedo olvidar lo que Cálgary ha dejado a un lado en su crecimiento, puesto que todo ello ha contribuido a lo que es hoy. Sin escombros no hay estructura.

Muchas de las fotografias de esta colección hablan por ellas mismas, reflejando mis sentimientos o ideas cuando las tome. A partir de ahora las dejo que hablen por mi; y si hacen su trabajo bien, como espero que lo hagan, ostras personas compartiran mis sentimientos por esta ciudad. Si esto ocurre, entonces he tenido éxito en presentar el Cálgary de Petrigo.

Зто была поездка на лошадях в трудный день. Я мог чувствовать скрип песка на зубах. Я коснулся бока моей лошади и в этом сухом пространстве поднялось маленькое облако пыли. Пора было отряду остановиться и отдохнуть.

Я думал, что это была обычная остановка, пока не подъехал к вершине холма, чтобы осмотреть местность. Она была прекрасной. Для солдата, который много испытал и видел, который создан так, чтобы восприниать только действительность, у которого нет времени воспринять поэзию и красоту, как таковые, это было захватывающее зрелище. Скалы блестели под лучами заходящего солнца, воды Боу и Злбоу обрамляли пышную долину, деревья вдоль берегов рек предлагали укрытие и мир.

Мы сделали привал и почувствовали себя, как дома.

Тоже самое, наверное почувствовали члены северо-западной конной полиции, которые впервые увидели и восприняли запад Канады, который впослествии должен. был стать городом Кадгари. Я приехад в Калгари много лет спустя - в 1951 году, но также почувствовад гостеприимство этого города. Не зная его, я нашел здесь свое место. Я слышал о Калгари всего за несколько месяцев до этого. Долгий путь поездром с восточной Канады дал много времени для работы моего воображения и я видел Калгари как след старой Англии, возможно с лендлордом-англичаниным, объезжающим свои поля и осматривающим работающих. Я также должен признаться, что имел немного представления о старом западе. Я не знал, что меня ждет.

То, что я нашел, когда сошел с поезда, было просто больше улыбок, или набольшие трудности в повседневных делах, таких, как открыть банку со сливками в Калгарийском ресторане, который я впервые посетил. В других отношениях Калгари нисколько не отличался от других больших городов мира.

Сегодня, для меня, Калгари мой дом, и он такой, как никакой другой город на свете. Если Вы спросите у меня, что делает этот город уникальным, то я отвечу, что это неправильный вопрос потому, чтот наш язык недостаточно богат, чтобы дать определение всем тем тонким чувствам, которые человек испытывает о своем доме. Для меня Калгари — исключительный город только потому, что Калгари — это перемешение людей, гор и прерий, вчерашнего и завтрашнего. Смешивая все эти характеристики я получаю Калгари.

Я вижу Калгари, как возможно наиболее обещаюший и волнующий город Канады, потому что в своем фундаменте он имеет довольно много тяжелых испытаний, довольно много непорочной чистоты потому, что он рос самопроизвольно, без стерильного плана. Первоначальный жизненный опыт, обычно самый трудный, и большинство калгарийцев привнесли пот этого первого опыта в среду, которую они называют домом.

Как люди, города тоже бывают старые и молодые. Калгари, как растущий молодой чеоловек, котроый удивляет самого себя своей только что обнаруженной силой и возможностями. Калгари, как юноша, который вырос из своих брюк — манжты где — то между лодыжками и коленками. Но голова юноши поднята вверх, он горд и смотрит вперед.

И каким-то образом, хотя сейчас мы являемся свидетелями больших перемен, я не думаю, что этот молодой город должен будет когда-либо оглядываться назад, потому что он повсюду содержит в себе надежды и возможноси молодых людей.

Изображать город, показывая только его здания,значит, в действительности, игнорировать наиболее важную часть этого города — людей и их реакции, их усилия, которые создали все эти сооружения. Я думаю, что лучше знать необходимость в этих постройках, чем просто видеть сооружения сами по себе.

Зто действительно правда, что люди являются самым большим богатством любого города, правдой является и то, что люди не приходят, как гиганты. Они приходят, как крупицы, прилаживаясь друг к другу, чтобы создать такое единое целое, которое отдельные крупицы нмкогда не могли себе представить. Как ребенок . . . старый человек . . . они все вносят свою лепту непредвиденным образом, создавая структуру города.

Калгари земной действительностью и имеет глубокие корни. Предполагается, что города должны расти определенно предписанным образом, но Калгари не имеет такого. Отдельные личности сделали его таким, как он есть . . . плавно, без натяжек, без модели, без этого разделения между тем, каким должен быть город и между тем, каким он есть. Калгари таков, каков он есть.

Несмотря на свою репутацию, это не город ковбоев. Мы любим придерживаться своего прошлого, и Праздник ковбоев Стампид является отражением этого желания, так что летом каждый становится ковбоем в течение 10 дней или около этого. Западный стиль сапог, которые мы одеваем и ковбойские шляпы, отражают желание в наших мыслях, которое не имеет отношения к практике. Мы хотим быть жителями запада, хотя бы на некоторое время, но время принесло свои изменения.

Праздник Стампид дает нам почувствоват прошлое. Вы можете набрести на фундамент Калгари, бродя вокруг холмов на распаханной земле. Вы можете все еще чувствовать смелые разговоры потомков пионеров. Вы можете почувствовать шершавые ладони, которые строили эту страну. Здесь вы также можете встретить рыцаря прошлого — высокого ковбоя, дотрагивающегося до своей шляпы, прося извинения у кого-то, кого он только что толкнул. Зто не сегодняшний Калгари, столица торговли и сельского хозяйства. Зто прошлое, пролитое в настоящее.

Калгари нельзя отсечь от окружающей территории потому, что эти окружающие его территории тоже делают его таким, каким он есть. Горы, прерии нефтяные промыслы, даже запах удобренной земли — все это Калгари.

В Калгари имеется наилучшее из двух миров — город и деревня. Здесь нет разделения. И так как этот город очень богат в своих рессурсах, он дает каждому возможность делать то, что он хочет. Как фотограф, я могу найти разновидности которые так необходимы, чтобы удовлетворить художественное любопытство — разновидность людей, разновидность архитектуры, разновидность пейзажей.

В этой книге я старался отразить эту разновидность, которая также включает этапы развития, через которые прошел этот город. Я хочу, чтобы книга была реальной, и, чтобы сделать это, я не могу забыть, что оставил Калгари на придорожной полосе, когда он развивался, так как это тоже дало свою лепту в сегодня. Без обломков нет постройки.

Много раз фотографии в этой коллекции будут молча говорить сами за себя, отражая то, что я чувствовал или понимал, когда я сам был частью фотографий. Сейчас их задача говорить за меня и, если они хорошо делают свое дело, так хорошо, как я надеюсь, тогда и другие люди смогут разделить то, что я знаю об этом городе. Если это получится, тогда я одержал успех, представляя Калгари Петриго.

Es war ein harter, den ganzen Tag dauernder Ritt. Ich fühlte den knirschenden Sand und Staub zwischen meinen Zähnen. Ich berührte die Flanke meines Pferdes, und in der Trockenheit stieg eine schmalle Staubwolke auf. Es war Zeit für die Einheit anzuhalten und sich auszuruhen.

Ich dachte, es würde eine normale Rast werden, bis ich zum Gipfel des Hügels ritt, um mir die Gegend anzuschauen. Sie war atemberaubend schön. Für einen Soldaten, der viel gesehen und erlebt hat, von dem nicht mehr erwartet wird, als dass er grundsätzliche Tatbestände begreift, der keine Zeit hatte, Dichtung und Schönheit für und in sich selbst zu verstehen, war es ein bewegender Anblick. Die Rockies erglänzten unter den Strahlen der untergehenden Sonne, die Gewässer des Bow und des Elbow umrahmten ein üppiges Tal, die Bäume entlang des Flusses boten Zuflucht und Frieden.

Wir errichteten das Lager und fühlten uns Zuhause.

So muss es für die Mitglieder der nordwestlichen berittenen Polizei gewesen sein, die zuerst die Gegend des kanadischen Westens, welche später die Stadt Calgary werden würde, erblickten und zu schätzen wussten. Ich selbst kam viele Jahre später nach Calgary — in 1951 — aber auch ich fühlte mich willkommen geheissen bei dieser Stadt. Ohne das ich es wusste, hatte ich mein Heim gefunden.

Zu diesem Zeitpunkt hatte ich nur einige Monate vorher zum erstenmal über Calgary gehört. Eine lange Reise mit dem Zug vom Osten Kanadas hatte meiner Vorstellungskraft mehr als genug Zeit gelassen sich zu betätigen, und ich sah Calgary vor meinem geistigen Auge als ein Rudiment des alten Englands; vielleicht sogar komplett mit einem englischen Gutsherrn, wie er über seine Felder ritt um seine Arbeiter zu beaufsichtigen. Ich muss auch gestehen, dass mir zudem Phantasien vom alten Wildwest vorschwebten. Ich wusste nicht, was ich zu erwarten hatte.

Was ich vorfand, nachdem ich aus dem Zug stieg, waren bescheidene, einfache Dinge — die Freundlichkeit und das Lächeln der Menschen, und kleine Probleme mit den alltäglichen

Dingen, wie zum Beispiel das Öffnen eines Milchbehälters in dem ersten Restaurant in Calgary, das ich besuchte. Ansonsten unterschied sich Calgary nicht besonders von anderen grossen Städten in der Welt.

Jetzt ist Calgary mein Zuhause, und es ist wie kein Platz sonst in der Welt. Sollten Sie mich fragen, was diese Stadt so einzigartig macht, würde ich antworten, dass dies eine unfaire Frage ist, da unsere Sprache nicht ausreicht, um all die Empfindungen auszudrücken, die ein Mensch für sein Heim empfindet. Für mich ist Calgary aussergewöhnlich, gerade weil es Calgary ist — eine bunte Mischung von Menschen, von Bergen und von Prärien, von Gestern und Heute. Diese Kombination von Attributen — das ist Calgary für mich.

Ich stelle mir Calgary als die vielversprechenste und lebendigste Stadt Kanadas vor. Die grundlegende Entwicklung Calgarys keimte aus seiner Periode des Mühsals, und auch aus seiner Unschuld während seines spontanen, ungeplanten und unberechenbaren Aufwachsens. Unmittelbare Erfahrungen sind normallerweise die schwersten; und die meisten Einwohner Calgarys fühlen sich durch den Schweiss dieser ersten Erfahrungen um so mehr mit ihrer Umgebung verbunden, welche sie ihr Heim nennen.

Wie Menschen können auch Städte alt oder jung sein. Calgary ist wie ein aufwachsender Bursche, ein Bursche, der sich selbst überrascht mit seiner noch unerkannten Stärke und seinem Potential. Calgary ist wie ein Jugendlicher, der aus seinen Hosen herausgewachsen ist — die Hosenaufschlage sitzen irgendwo zwischen den Fesseln und den Knien. Aber dieser Jugendliche hält seinen Kopf hoch; er ist stolz und schaut nach vorn. Und irgendwie, selbst während der Veränderungen, die wir jetzt erleben, glaube ich nicht, dass diese junge Stadt jemals zurückblicken wird, da es die Hoffnung und die Entwicklungsfähigkeit aller Jugendlichen besitzt.

Diese Stadt nur durch seine Bauten zu porträtieren, heisst wirklich den wichsten Bestandteil dieser Stadt zu übergehen — ihr Menschen und ihre Reaktionen, ihre Bemühungen, welche diese Bauten erschaffen haben. Ich glaube, es ist besser über die Notwendigkeit für und das Bedürfnis nach diesen Bauten Bescheid zu wissen, als nur die Strukturen in sich selbst zu betrachten.

Obwohl es stimmt, dass Menschen das höchste Gut in jedweder Stadt darstellen, stimmt es ebenso, dass Menschen als Einzelpersonen keine Riesen sind. Sie sind schmalle Einheiten, die sich in- und aneinander anpassen, um ein Ganzes zu bilden, dass bei weitem mehr darstellt, als die Teile sich selbst jemals vorstellen konnten. Auf diese Weise trägt das Kind . . . der alte Mann . . . sie alle tragen in unerwarteter Art und Weise dazu bei, die Struktur der Stadt zu erschaffen.

Calgary besitzt einen immer gegenwärtigen Realitätssinn, welcher dem Boden entstammt und der tief verwurzelt ist. Von Städten wird erwartet, dass sie in bestimmter und vorgeschriebener Art und Weise wachsen, aber Calgary tat es nicht. Individuelle Kreationen erschuffen es wie es ist . . . fliessend, mühelos, ohne eine Schablone zu benutzen, ohne die Spaltung zwischen was eine Stadt sein sollte, und was sie in Wirklichkeit ist. Calgary ist, was es ist.

Es ist nicht eine Cowboystadt, trotz ihres Rufes. Wir wollen an unserem Erbgut festhalten, und die Stampede reflektiert dieses Verlangen; und so verwandelt sich jedermann im Sommer in einen Cowboy fur ungefähr zehn Tage. Die Westernstiefel und der Cowboyhut, die wir tragen, reflektieren eine Sehnsucht in unserer Seele, welche keine Verbindung mit dem Praktischen hat. Wir wollen den alten Westen repräsentieren, zumindest für eine Weile, aber Zeit hat ihre Veränderungen erzwungen.

Aber so gibt uns die Stampede ein Gefühl für die Vergangenheit. Sie können hinter den Rodeopferchen, in denen die wilden Pferde und Stiere vorübergehend vor dem Rodeowettkampf gehalten werden, entlanggehen und hier die Grundlagen von Calgary wiederfinden. Sie können nach wie vor die derben und handfesten Gespräche und Sprache der Nachkommen der Pioniere hören. Sie können dort den Drang und das Ungestüm wiederfinden, die dieses Land aufgebaut haben. Und dort können Sie auch die Ritterlichkeit der Vergangenheit finden — ein grossgewachsener Cowboy lüftet entschuldigend seinen Hut vor jemanden, den er gerade vorher angestossen hat. Dies ist nicht das Calgary von heute, das Zentrum von Wirtschaft und Landwirtschaft. Dies ist die Vergangenheit, die in die Gegenwart hinüberreicht.

Calgary kann nicht kontextlos gesehen werden, da das es umgebene Land dazu beiträgt, was est ist. Berge, Prärien, Ölfelder, selbst der Geruch des fruchtbaren Bodens — all diese Güter repräsentieren Calgary.

Calgary hat das Beste beider Welten — Stadt und Land. Da gibt es keine Trennung. Und da die Stadt so reich an Rohmaterialien ist, erlaubt sie allen das zu erstreben, was es auch immer sein mag, dass sie wirklich tun möchten. Als Photograph kann ich hier die Vielfaltigkeit finden, die so nötig ist für eines Künstlers Wissbegierde — eine Vielfalt von Menschen, Vielfalt in Architektur, Abwechslung in der Landschaft.

In diesem Buch habe ich versucht, diese Mannigfaltigkeit wiederzugeben, eine Vielfalt, die ebenso die verschieden Phasen der Entwicklung miteinschliesst, durch die diese Stadt gelebt hat. Ich habe versucht, durch dieses buch die Realität, wie sie ist, wiederzugeben, und um das zu tun, darf ich nicht vergessen, was Calgary hinter sich gelassen hat, während die Stadt erwachsen wurde, da auch das zu dem Heute beiträgt. Bei dem Bau eines Gebäudes oder einter grösseren Struktur muss auch Schutt entstehen.

Die Photos in dieser Kollektion werden oft für sich selbst sprechen, ohne das Worte von Nöten sind; sie spiegeln wieder, was ich selbst fühlte und begriff, wenn ich selbst ein Bestandteil des Photos war. Von jetzt an tragen diese Bilder die Verantwortung für den Ausdruck meiner Person, und sollten sie erfolgreich darin sein, was ich hoffe, dann wird es meinen Mitmenschen möglich sein, mein Begreifen dieser Stadt zu teilen. Sollte dies geschehen, dann habe ich Ihnen Petrigos Calgary vorgestellt.

馬での旅 ― それは辛いものであった。口の中は埃でざらざらし、馬の横腹にさわってみると、そこは乾燥して、埃が立ちのぼる程であった。丁度、休憩の時間になった。

それは、廻りの景色を見るために見晴らし台まで馬を進めるまでは、極く普通の休息のつもりだったが、そこに着いてみると、素晴らしい眺望だった。幾多の見聞と経験を重ねたが、現実以外の予を理解できない。また、詩とか美の世界を享受する時間を持てない兵士にとっては、それは、とても感動的な眺めであった。ロッキー山脈は残照に映え、ボー川、エルボー川の 2つの川が水々しく茂った渓谷を囲み、両川にそった木々は憩と平和を漂わせていた。

我々はキャンプを張って、貴い気分に浸ったのである。

後年カルガリー市となったカナダ西部の地を最初に見、感嘆したのは北西騎馬警察隊員だったと思われる。私はずっと後年、1951年にカルガリーに着いた時、この町が私を歓迎してくれるのを感じた。そんなこととは知らずに、私はこの地を偶然に発見したのである。

当時、私は僅か数ヶ月前にカルガリーの事を耳にしたばかりであった。東部カナダからの汽車の長旅の間、私は想像をめぐらせていた。私は心の中に古い英国の名残り ― おそらく英国の地主が小作人を監督して農場を馬でかけめぐっている様な風景 ― をとどめる地としてカルガリーを思い描いていた。又、古い西部の町としてのカルガリーを想像していたのでもある。実際のところ、どんな期待をしてよいのかわからなかった。

汽車が止まり、私の目にうつったのは、純粋で素朴な事柄であった。私がカルガリーで最初に訪れたレストランでは、人々は他所よりも もっと

25

微笑をたたえていたし、問題といえば、クリームの容器をどう開けるかと言った様の些細な事柄であった。さもなければ、カルガリーは世界中のどんな町とも変るところがないように思われた。

現在、カルガリーは私の故郷となった。こんな素晴らしい町は世界に二つとさえないと思える。どうしてこの町がユニークなのかと尋ねられたら、私はそれは野暮な質問だと答えるだろう。なぜならば、どんな言葉をあてはめてもその時の私の気持を言いつくせない程、素晴らしい所だからである。私にとってカルガリーとは、市民と自然が渾然一体となった姿、過去と未来の良さが一体となったが故にユニークな町なのである。

私はカルガリーはカナダで最も将来性と活力に富んだ町だと思う。なぜなら、カルガリーは過去の素朴さを残しながら、かつ発展を遂げてきたからである。最初に得た経験というものは通常最も苛酷なものである。大部分のカルガリー市民はその最初の経験という汗の結晶を縮等が故郷と呼ぶ環境に溶け込ませていたのである。

人間同様、町にも老若がある。カルガリーは成長中の若者の様に躍進と将来性に富んでいるのである。仮にたとえるなら、カルガリーは、自分の洋服が小さくなってしまった若者である。ズボンの丈は短かくなってしまたが、顔は上を向き、誇に満ちて前途を見つめている若者である。そして我々が今、体験しつつある時代の流れを見ても、この若い都市が後戻りすることはないと思われる。何故ならば、この町全体に若者のもつ希望と未来が溢れているからである。

ある町を表現するのに、その町の連物だけを言うのは、その町全体を説明していることにはならない。—その土地の人間と、縮等の行動。

あらゆる建造物を築き上げた彼等の努力なしには語れないのである。単に建物のみを見るよりも、それら建物の快適性を知る方の方が重要だと私は思う。

どんな都市においても人間が最も重要な資産であることは事実だが、人間が巨人であり得ないことも事実である。人間は1個の単位であり、部分からは想像し得ない全体を創造するために各々が協力するのである。かくして子供も老人も全てが町の建設に思わぬ方法で貢献することになるのである。

カルガリーは地中から湧き出る活力を持っている。都会というものは定められた方向に発展していくと思われているがカルガリーの場合はそうではない。個々の市民が今のカルガリーを作ったのである。雄弁に、ひずみなく、型にとらわれず、市のあるべき姿と現実の姿の間の乖離もなく、カルガリーはありのままの姿で存在する。

カルガリーはよく知られる通りのカウボーイの町ではない。我々は歴史の遺産を受け継ぎたい。スタンピード祭はその願望の表われである。それ故、夏の10日ばかりは全市民がカウボーイになるのである。ウエスターンブーツやカウボーイハットは我々の胸中にある欲求を反映するもので、実用性とは何らの関係もない。我々はほんの僅かの間だけでもウエスタンに戻りたい。しかし時代は変ったのだ。

しかしながら、あのスタンピード祭は我々の過去を偲ばせてくれる。農場のシュートの辺りを歩いてみると、そこに昔のカルガリーの面影が偲れる。今でも開拓者達の子孫の不屈の物語を聞くことができるだろう。この国を築き上げた雄々しさも見つけられるだろう。又、そこでは過去の郷土愛にもお目にかかれるかもしれない。長身のカウボーイが他人に

27

ぶつかた時に 詫りに カウボーイハットに手をあてるゼスチャーが それである。
これは今のカルガリーではない。商業農業の中心地としてのカルガリーではない。
これは現在に持ちこされた過去にすぎないのである。

　カルガリーはその周辺地域と切り離して言ることは不可能で
ある。何故なら、その周辺地域も今のカルガリーの一部を成している
からである。山脈、平原、油田、そして肥沃な土地の臭いすらもすべて
が カルガリーなのである。

　カルガリーは 都会と田舎の2つの長所を合せ持っている。この間
に境はない。この市は豊富な資源に恵まれている故に、誰もが自分の欲
するものに手を伸ばすことが出来る。写真家としての私は、芸術的好奇心
を満足させるに必要な多用性を見つけ出すことが出来る。一人間、事業
風景等 諸々のバラエティーが それである。

　この本の中で 私はこの市が経験した 開発・発展の段階
と示す多用性を表現しようと試みた。私はこの本が現実性を帯びた
ものであることを企図し、そのために発展段階でこの市が路傍にのこして
きたものを忘れることができない。何故なら、それも又 今のカルガリーを
創り上げるのに貢献したからである。車等も石礫もまた、必要なように。

　このコレクションの中の写真は、静かに繰り返して語りかけてくれる
であろう。それは私自身がその写真の一部であった時に感じ、あるいは
理解したことを語ってくれることに 他ならない。これからは、私に代って
語ってくれるのが これら写真の責任であり、もし 私の望み通り、
この任務をうまく果してくれれば、他の人をも、私のこの市への理解に
共鳴してくれるだろう。その時、はじめて、私は「ペルティグのカルガリー」
を紹介することに 成功したことになるのである。

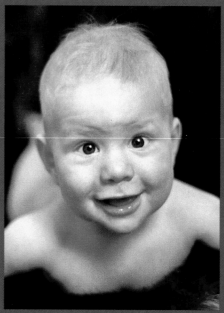

Dear SCHOOLBOARD,
I'll gladly teach all about
the OLYMPICS, IF we
can have the THREE WEEKS
OFF, (including THE "KIOZ"
(HOORAY)!! -to enjoy this ONCE
IN-A-LIFETIME EXPERIENCE,
FIRSTHAND!! XOXOXOXOX
A DEDICATED TEACHER,
(and SIGN-PAINTER),
JOYCE ROBBINS

39

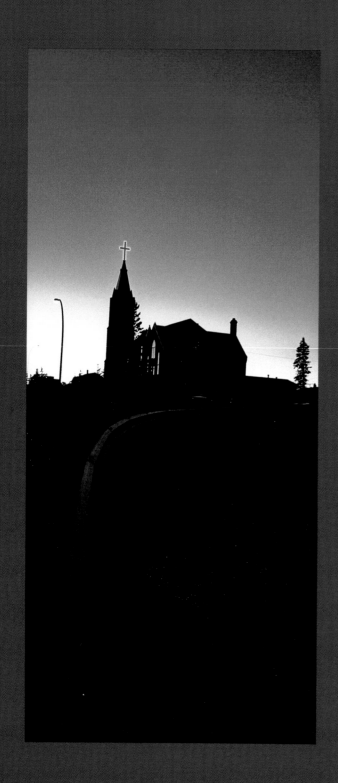

60

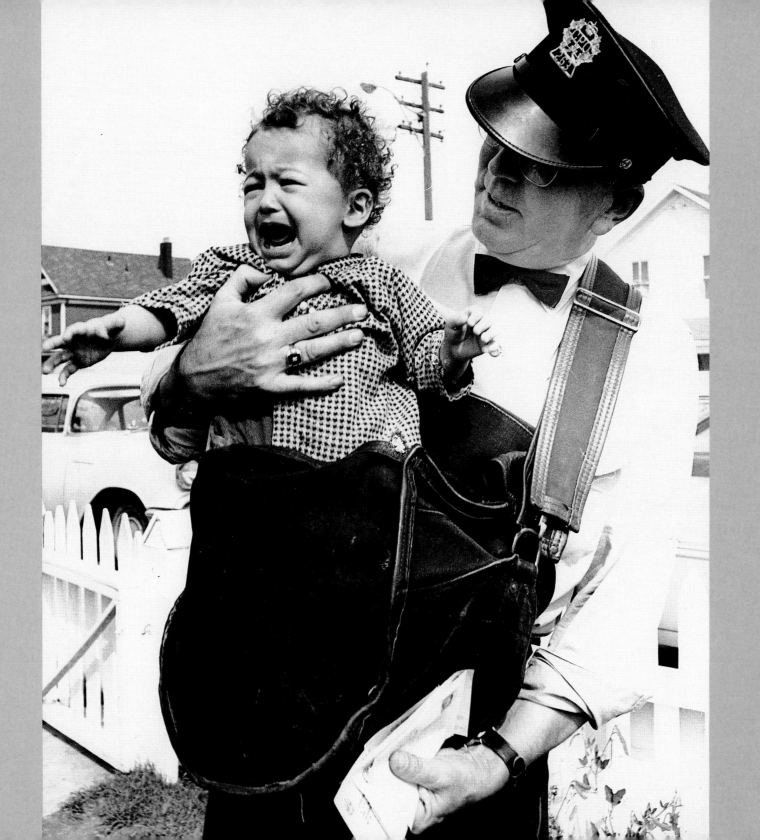

78

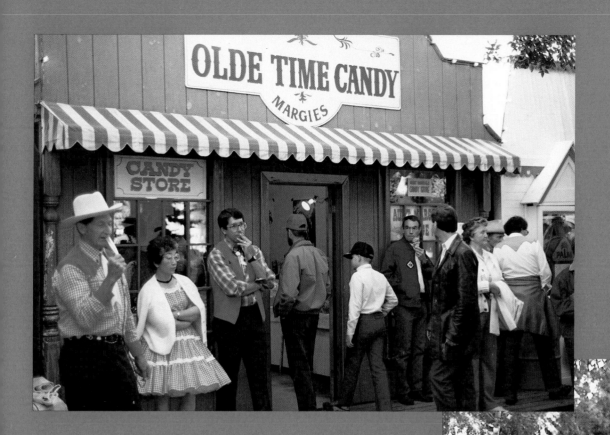

1962

1987

1962

1987

115

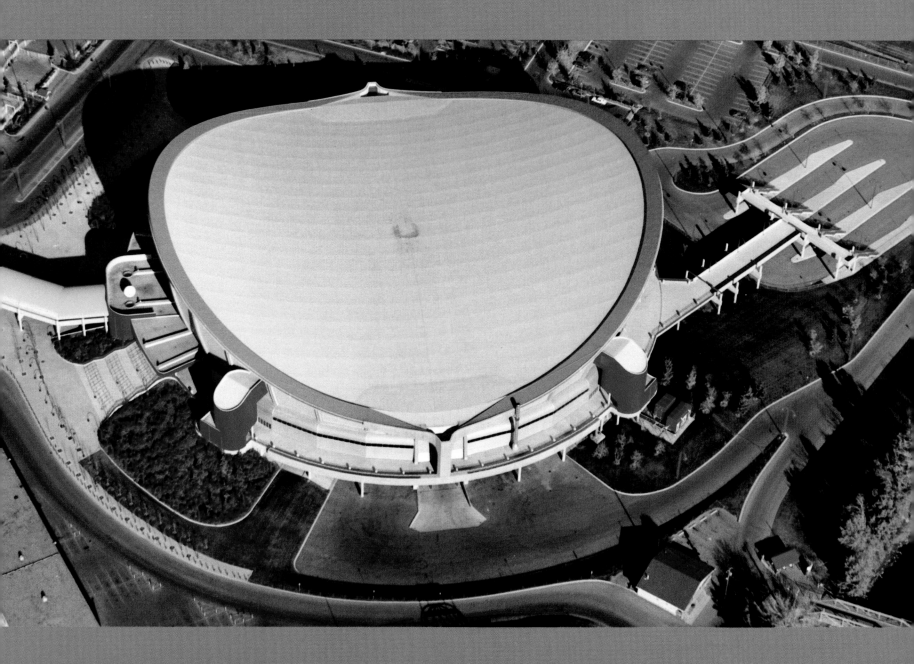

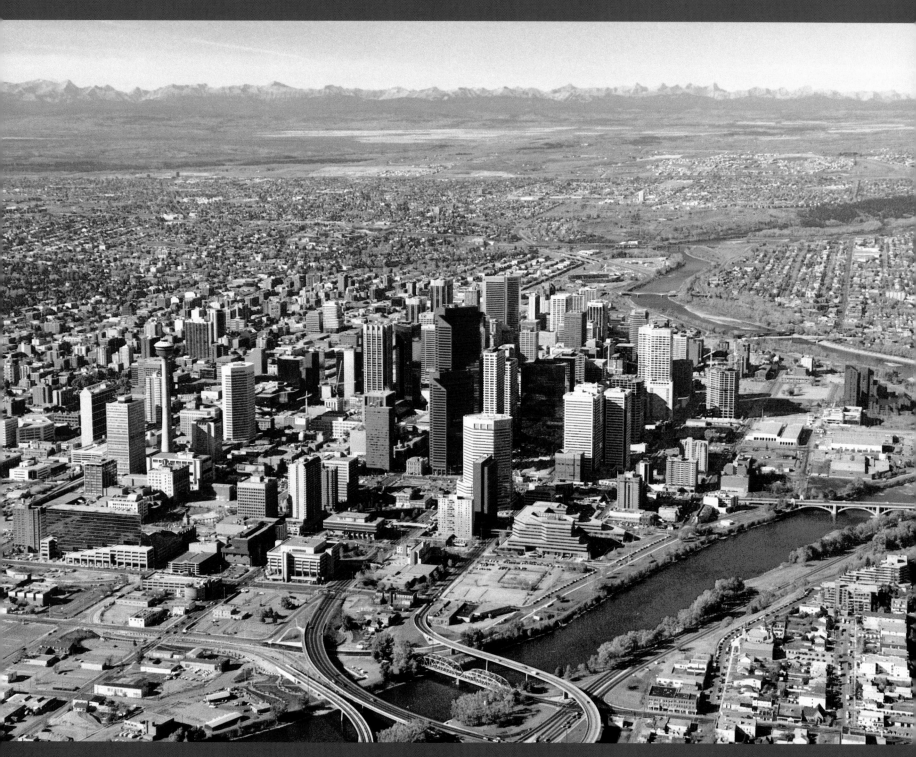

144

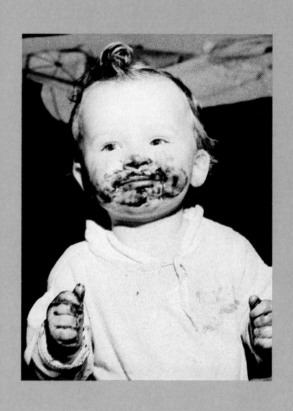

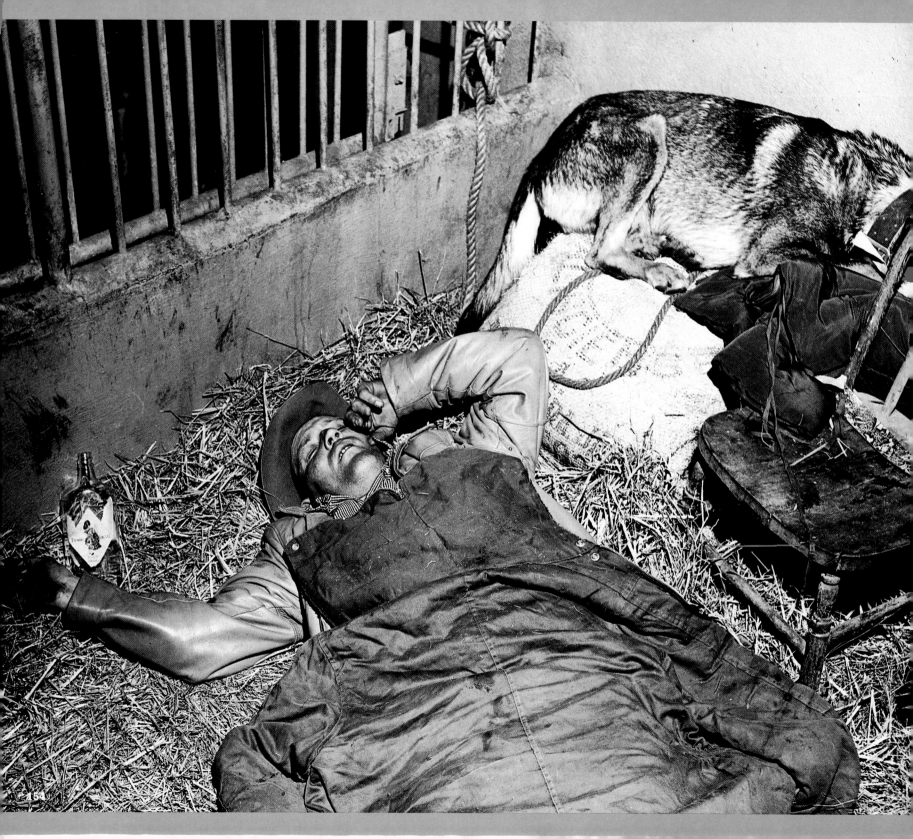

155

INDEX